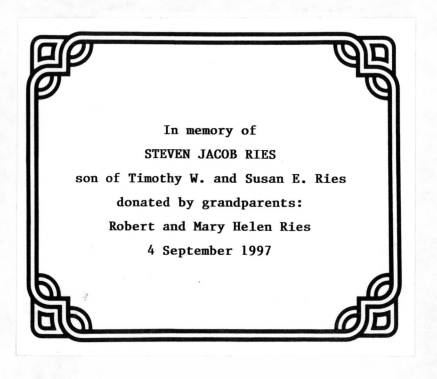

In memory of
STEVEN JACOB RIES
son of Timothy W. and Susan E. Ries
donated by grandparents:
Robert and Mary Helen Ries
4 September 1997

A Tractor
Goes Farming

Roy Harrington

**Published by the
American Society of Agricultural Engineers
2950 Niles Road, St. Joseph, Michigan**

Photo Credits
John Deere: front cover, 4, 5, 7, 8, 11, 15, 21.
New Holland: 3, 12, 14, 16, 17, 22.
Case IH: 6, 9, 13, 31 upper, 31 lower, back cover.
Wylie: 10. DMI: 18. Kinze: 19. Krause: 20. Gehl: 23.
Massey-Ferguson (AGCO): 24. White-New Idea (AGCO): 25.
BUSH HOG®: 26. Servis-Rhino: 27. Danuser: 28. Alloway: 29.
Don Brummel: 30.

A Tractor Goes Farming
Editor: Richard Balzer
Project Manager: Melissa Carpenter

Library of Congress Cataloging-in Publication Data
Harrington, Roy
A Tractor Goes Farming

Summary: Tractor and implement use on farms throughout
the year is given in photos and simple text.
1. Tractors – Juvenile literature. 2. Agricultural Machinery –
   Juvenile literature. 3. Farms – Juvenile literature.
[1. Tractors. 2. Agricultural Machinery] I. Title.
   TL123.H45   1995   631.3   95-54321
ISBN 0-929355-68-7
LCCN 95-77925

Printed in the United States

A Tractor Goes Farming

Roy Harrington

A tractor pulls a plow
to turn over the soil.

A tractor uses a field cultivator
to prepare the soil for planting.

A tractor uses a grain drill
to plant wheat or soybeans.

A tractor pulls a planter
to plant corn, cotton, or soybeans.

A tractor uses a rotary hoe
to uproot weeds in a soybean field.

A tractor uses a cultivator
to dig weeds between vegetable rows.

A tractor powers a sprayer
to kill bugs on cotton plants.

A tractor powers a mower
to cut grass hay for cattle feed.

A tractor pulls a rake
to gather mowed hay into a row.

A tractor pulls a mower-conditioner to cut, condition, and gather hay.

A tractor powers a square baler
to pack alfalfa hay into bales.

A tractor powers a round baler
to roll up large bales of hay.

A tractor powers a forage harvester to chop corn silage for cattle feed.

A tractor powers a forage blower
to send silage up into a storage silo.

A tractor pulls a gravity flow wagon to haul soybeans from a combine.

A tractor powers a grain cart
to unload corn shelled by a combine.

A tractor pulls a disk
to cut stalks after combining.

A tractor pulls a chisel plow
to loosen the soil.

A tractor powers a grinder-mixer
to make and deliver feed to hogs.

A tractor powers a mixer-feeder
to stir and deliver feed to cattle.

A tractor scoops with a farm loader
to clean a cattle pen.

A tractor powers a spreader
to fertilize a field with cattle manure.

A tractor powers a rotary cutter
to cut tall weeds.

A tractor drags a rear blade
to smooth a gravel road.

A tractor powers a posthole digger to drill holes for fence posts.

A tractor powers a snow blower
to clear snow from a road.

A tractor pulls a wagon
to give children a hayride.

A tractor has many parts
designed by people called engineers.

About the Author

Roy Harrington grew up on a livestock and grain farm. He worked more than 30 years as an engineer planning and developing John Deere farm equipment. Roy is co-author of *John Deere Tractors and Equipment 1960-1990*, a best seller farm equipment history book. His five grandchildren are fascinated by all his tractors, from the smallest toy to the largest of the three real tractors he drives.

About ASAE — The Society for engineering in agricultural, food, and biological systems

ASAE is a technical and professional organization committed to improving agriculture through engineering. Many of our 8,000 members in the United States, Canada, and more than 100 other countries are engineering professionals actively involved in designing the farm equipment that continues to help the world's farmers feed the growing population. We're proud of the triumphs of the agriculture and equipment industry.